DAILY TRUTH

SCRIPTURE TO MEDITATE ON
IN EVERY CIRCUMSTANCE

KRISTIN SCHMUCKER
& SARAH MORRISON

TOPICS

HE DOESN'T
LEAVE US TO SUFFER
IN OUR WORRY
AND ANXIETY

ANXIETY & WORRY

Anxiety can haunt us. It can tear us away from our relationships with others and God if we allow it to. But most of all, anxiety lies to us. Anxiety tells us that God is not in control and that His plans are not good. But God does not leave us to suffer in our worry and anxiety alone. Instead, He gives us Himself. It may seem trite to think that something that can plague us so much could be transformed by prayer, petition, and thinking of God, but we know and trust God's Word to be true. He can and does work through our anxiety to bring us closer to Him.

Lay your anxieties at His feet, take up His good Word, and fix your eyes to the One who finishes and perfects our faith.

ANXIETY & WORRY

JOHN 14:27

MATTHEW 6:25-34

MATTHEW 11:28-30

1 PETER 5:7

PHILIPPIANS 4:6-7

PHILIPPIANS 4:19

PROVERBS 3:5-6

PSALM 9:10

PSALM 23:4

PSALM 28:7

PSALM 37:5

PSALM 55:22

PSALM 94:19

2

ANGER

Anger can consume us and tear us away from those we love. God exemplifies perfectly righteous anger. However, we are imperfect, sinful humans, and it is a struggle to only be angry in righteous ways. Anger is a problem when it convinces us that we are more important than those who anger us or when we allow it to produce bitterness and resentment within us. Instead, Jesus models for us a meek spirit, He loves others relentlessly, and praises God in all things.

Sinful anger can be difficult to overcome, but when we flee from our unrighteous anger, we are conformed to His image all the more.

COLOSSIANS 3:8

ECCLESIASTES 7:9

EPHESIANS 4:31

JAMES 1:19-20

JAMES 4:1-2

LUKE 6:31

1 PETER 2:23

PROVERBS 15:1

PROVERBS 15:18

PROVERBS 16:32

PSALM 37:8

PSALM 86:15

ROMANS 12:21

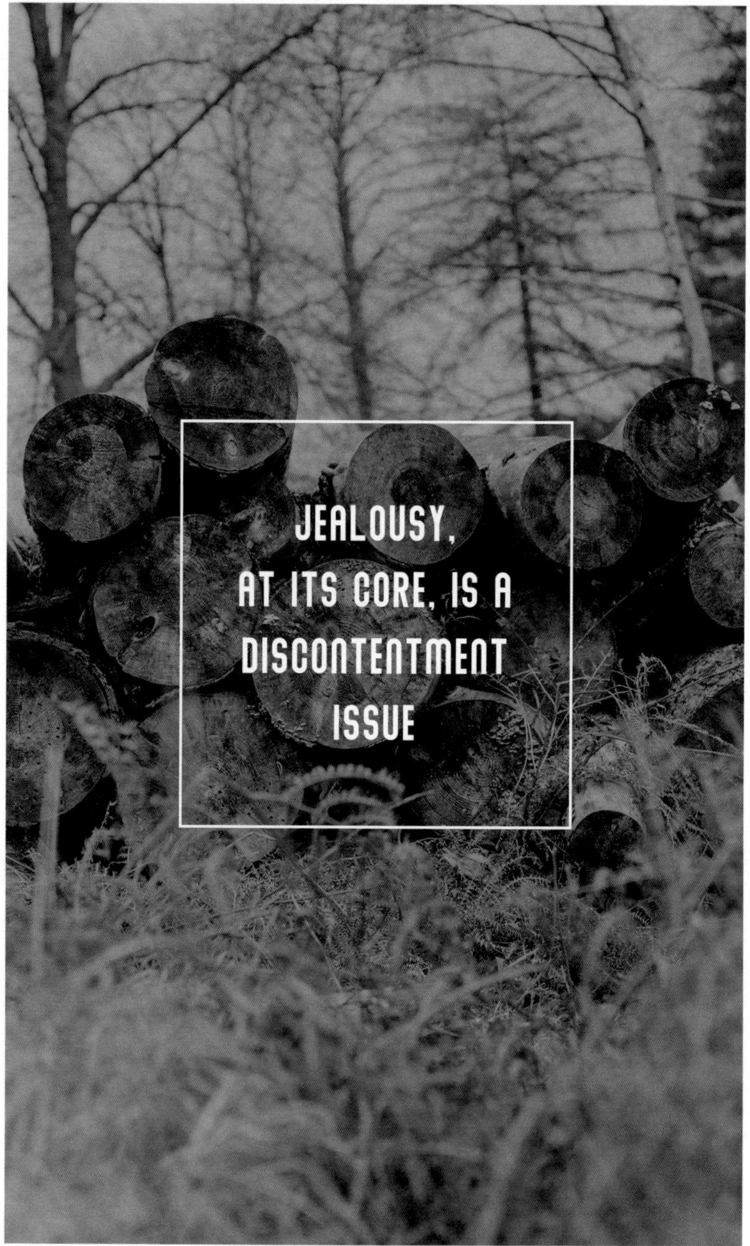
JEALOUSY,
AT ITS CORE, IS A
DISCONTENTMENT
ISSUE

JEALOUSY & CONTENTMENT

Jealousy, at its core, is a discontentment issue. We grow jealous and discontent when we believe that we are deserving of far more than what God has granted us and when we look at what others have and decide that they are far less deserving than we are. Jealousy is a liar. Our God supplies our every need, and He does so with great compassion and grace. The art of contentment grows from focusing on Jesus Christ, knowing that He is entirely sufficient for all of our needs and our wants.

Lay before Him all of your desires, and He will supply you with riches of Himself that will last you forever.

JEALOUSY & CONTENTMENT

I CORINTHIANS 13:4

EPHESIANS 5:20

HEBREWS 13:5

JAMES 3:14-18

LUKE 12:15

MATTHEW 6:25-26

PHILIPPIANS 4:19

PROVERBS 3:5-6

PROVERBS 14:30

PROVERBS 28:25

PSALM 37:1-3

PSALM 37:7

I THESSALONIANS 5:18

I TIMOTHY 6:6

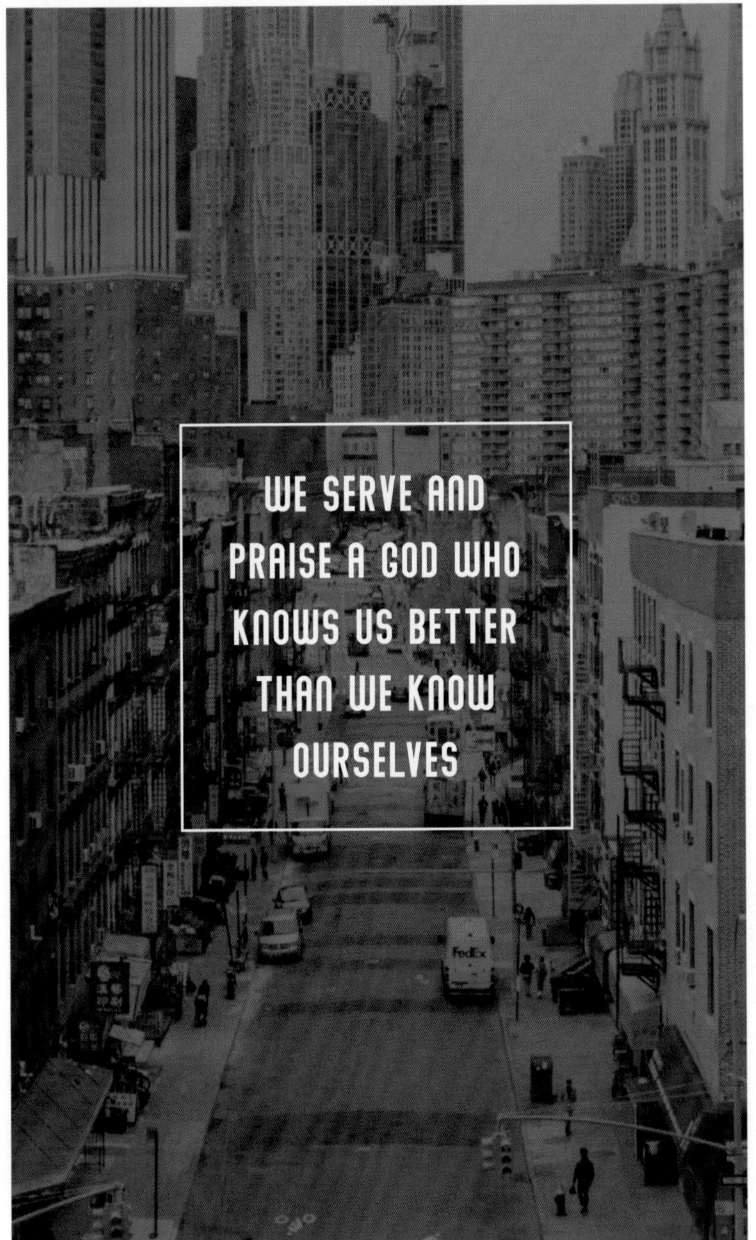
WE SERVE AND PRAISE A GOD WHO KNOWS US BETTER THAN WE KNOW OURSELVES
FedEx

FEELING UNLOVED

We often feel unloved and alone when we rely on the world's love, love from mere men and women, friends and family. People will always fail us, but we have a God who will always love us with an unrelenting, unfailing love. We serve and praise a God who loved us enough to give Himself up for us, to die on a cross the death that we deserve. We serve and praise a God who gives us the full story of Scripture, a story that tells us of His deep love and desire to dwell with His people in a way that resembles a pre-fall Eden. We serve and praise a God who knows us better than we know ourselves. He knows all the filthiness of our souls but still loves, cares, and provides for us.

God's love is good, and it is more than enough to satisfy us.

EPHESIANS 2:4-7

EPHESIANS 3:17-19

ISAIAH 54:10

I JOHN 4:12-19

JOHN 3:16

JOHN 15:13

LAMENTATIONS 3:22-23

PSALM 18:19

PSALM 40:17

PSALM 136:1

ROMANS 5:8

ROMANS 8:38-39

ZEPHANIAH 3:17

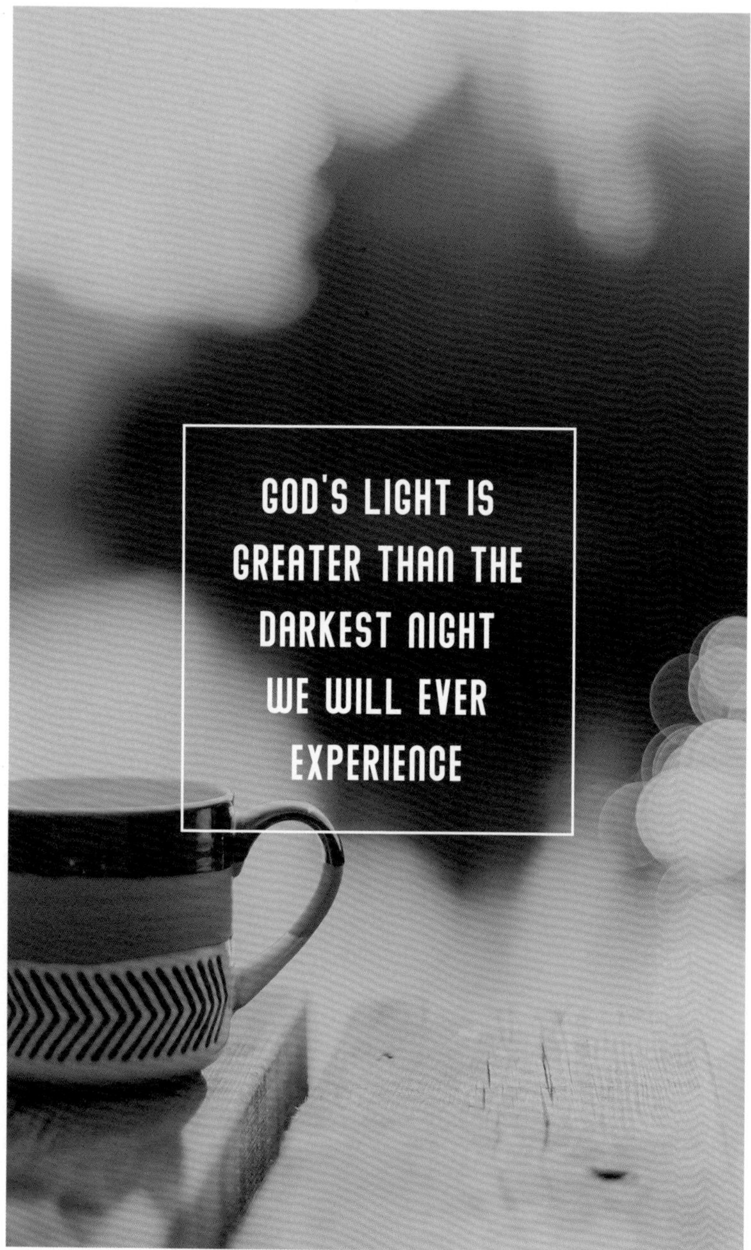
GOD'S LIGHT IS
GREATER THAN THE
DARKEST NIGHT
WE WILL EVER
EXPERIENCE

FEAR

Fear is almost tangible in our lives. Fear tempts us to believe that our God is not as strong as the things in this world, but the very Word of God assures us that He is all-powerful. God's light is greater than the darkest night we will ever experience. We can be certain and confident that the Lord is at hand, that He is working, and that He is overcoming the frightening things of this world with His marvelous light. In Him, we do not have to be afraid. In Him, there is no need to seek refuge in the things of the world.

In Him, we are safe, secure, and protected.

FEAR

DEUTERONOMY 3:22

ISAIAH 41:10

ISAIAH 41:13-14

ISAIAH 43:1

1 JOHN 4:18

JOHN 14:27

PSALM 23:4

PSALM 27:1

PSALM 34:4

PSALM 46:1-3

PSALM 55:22

PSALM 56:3-4

PSALM 91

2 TIMOTHY 1:7

WHEN WE ARE FEELING LONELY OR FORSAKEN, WE CAN LOOK TO CHRIST

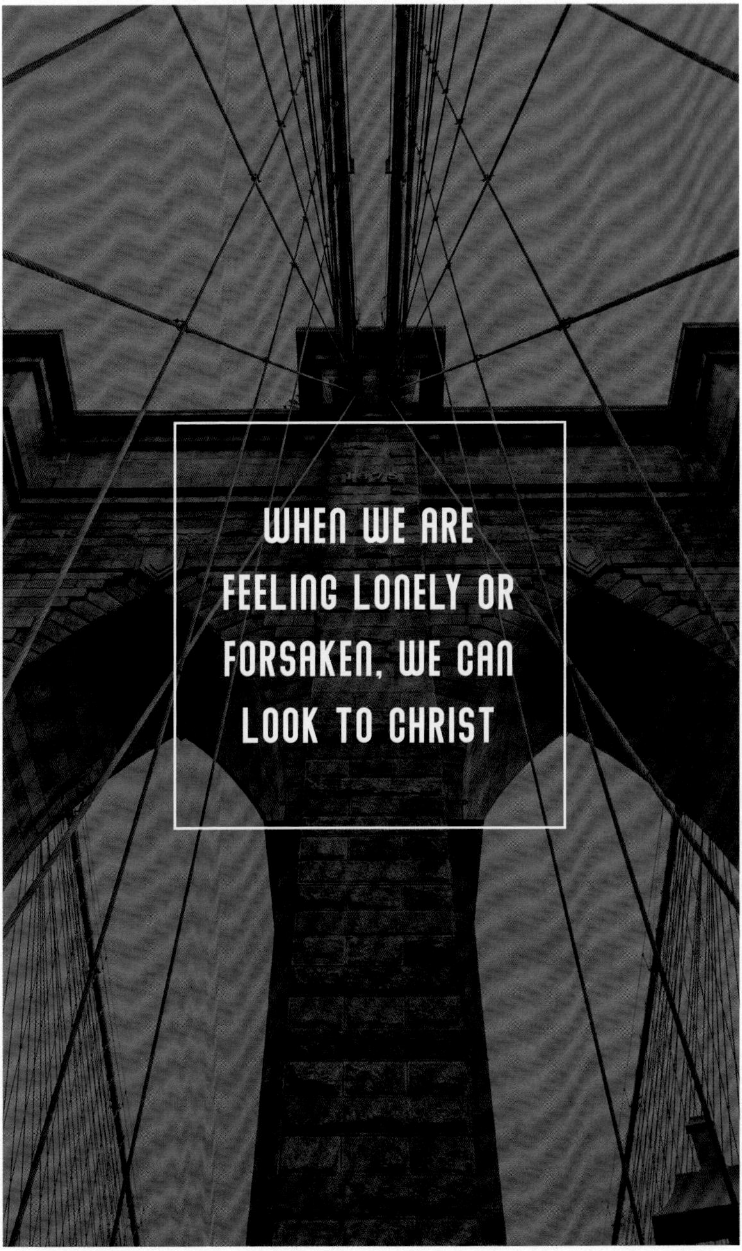

LONELINESS

Satan and his workers love to use loneliness as a tool to distract and disarm us. Loneliness can be depleting and cause us to forget the friendship that the Lord offers us without fail. Other people will forsake us, but we can rest in the certainty that God will never withhold Himself from us. When we are feeling lonely or forsaken, we can look to Christ, knowing that he endured every bit of suffering that we experience. We know that He understands and sympathizes with us in our pain.

When we feel alone and dejected, we can be sure that God Himself is with us.

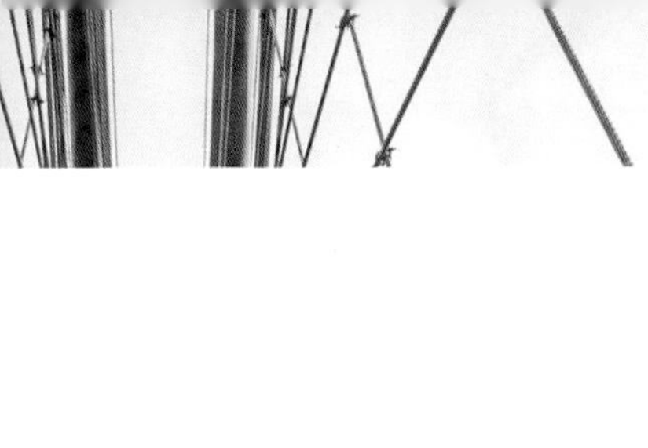

DEUTERONOMY 31:8

HEBREWS 13:6

ISAIAH 41:10

ISAIAH 43:2

JOHN 14:16-18

JOHN 15:15

JOSHUA 1:5

MATTHEW 28:20

PSALM 16:8

PSALM 73:23-26

PSALM 119:114

PSALM 120:1

PSALM 139:7-10

REVELATION 21:3

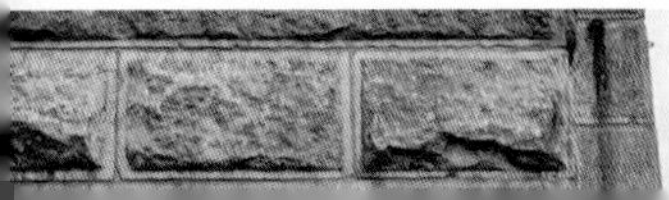

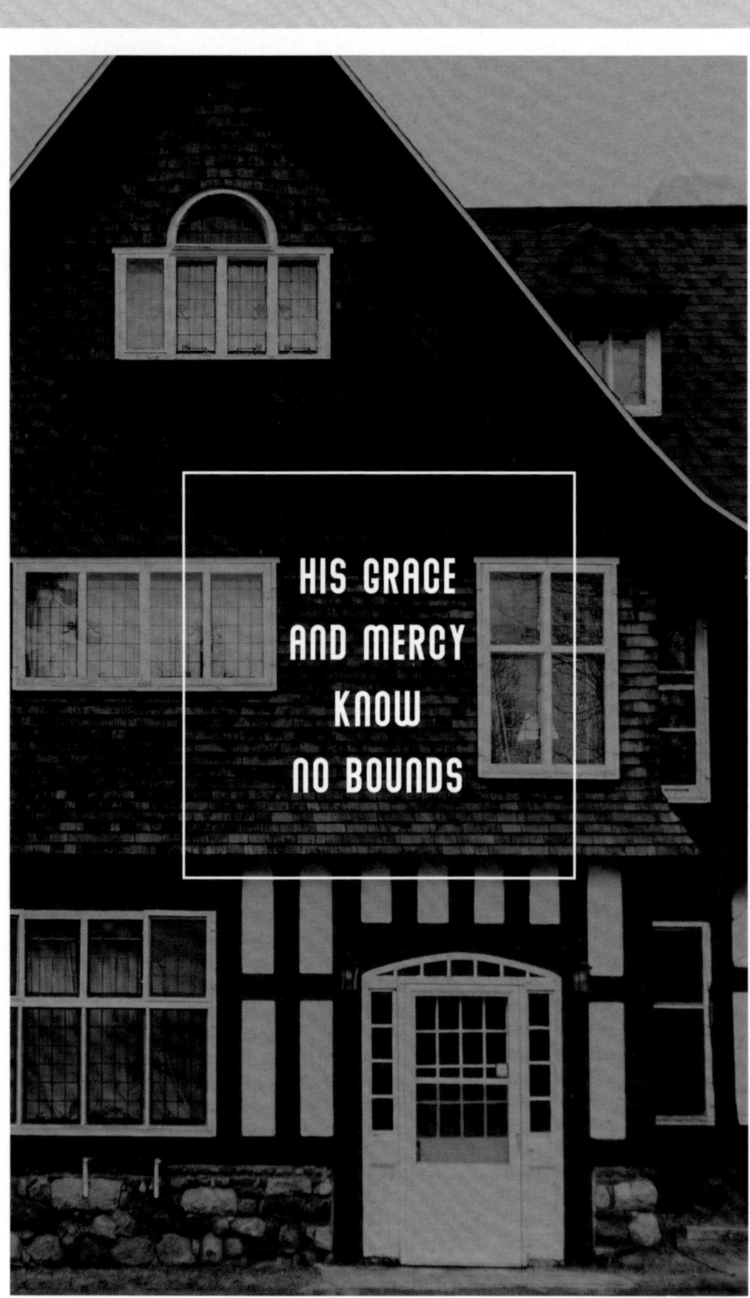
HIS GRACE
AND MERCY
KNOW
NO BOUNDS

BROKEN-HEARTEDNESS

So many things can cause a broken heart within us, and for every single one of those causes, we know that Jesus Christ offers healing. There is no limit to His healing power. His grace and mercy know no bounds, and His care for His people is indiscriminate. He will always provide you with healing through a relationship with Him. There are no harsh words that He cannot mend. There are no cruel intentions that He cannot redeem.

He is always able to move us from a broken heart to a joyful heart, and He delights in proving Himself to us over and over again.

BROKEN-HEARTEDNESS

2 CORINTHIANS 12:9

ISAIAH 43:1

ISAIAH 61:1

JEREMIAH 29:11

JOHN 16:33

PROVERBS 3:5-6

PSALM 9:9

PSALM 22:24

PSALM 34:18

PSALM 56:8

PSALM 62:8

PSALM 73:26

PSALM 147:3

ROMANS 8:18

ROMANS 8:28

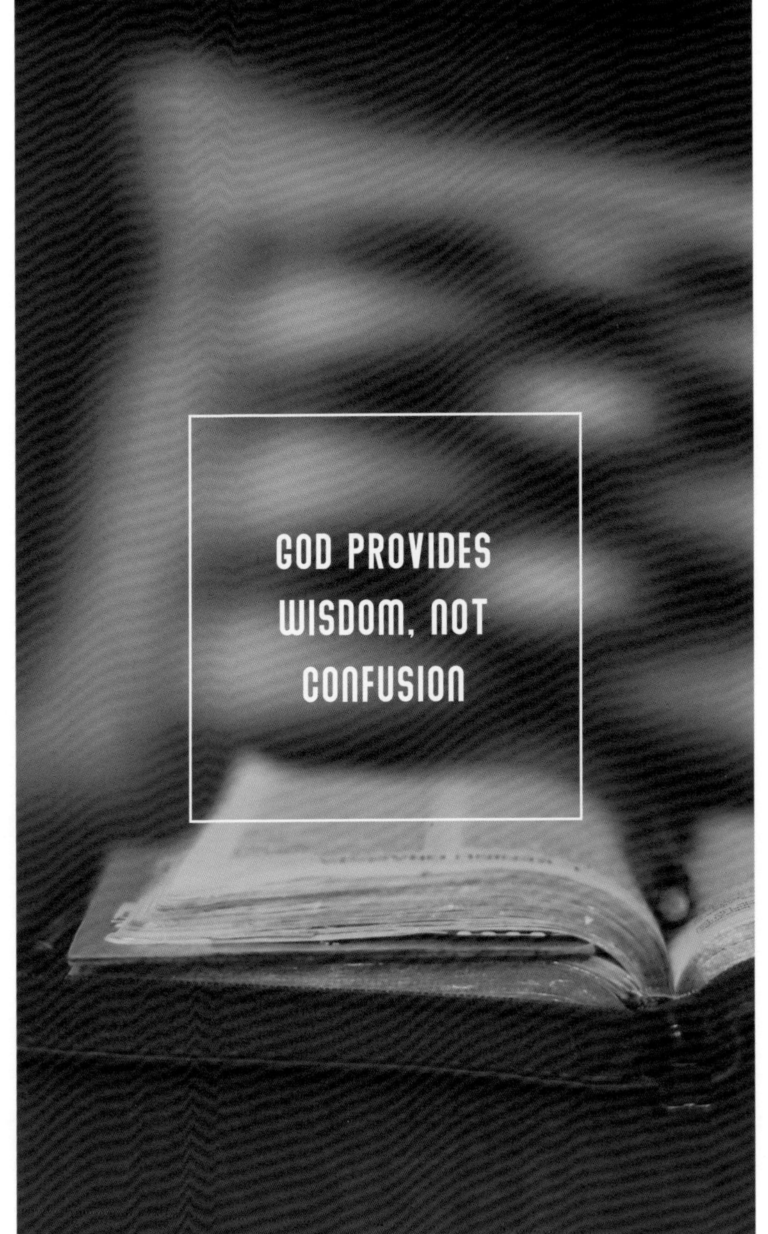
GOD PROVIDES
WISDOM, NOT
CONFUSION

CONFUSION

God provides wisdom, not confusion. Praise God that He will never withhold wisdom from us when we ask Him! We will always have limited knowledge because only God is all-knowing, but God gives us all the knowledge we need for life and godliness. When we are overwhelmed by confusion, we can stand firm in the knowledge that the Holy Spirit will guide and direct our thoughts as we commune with Him through His Word.

The all-knowing God has given us all we need in Scripture.

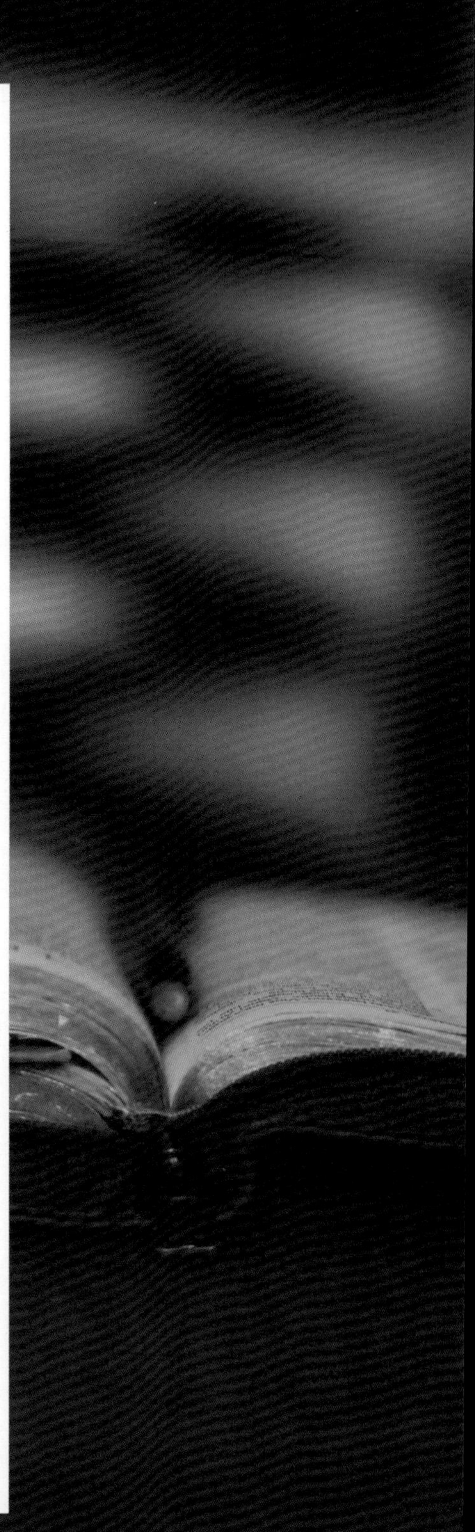

I CORINTHIANS 1:30

I CORINTHIANS 14:33

HEBREWS 13:8

ISAIAH 40:28

ISAIAH 55:8

JAMES 1:5

JAMES 3:17

JOHN 16:33

MATTHEW 7:7

PHILIPPIANS 4:8-9

PROVERBS 2:6

PSALM 119:34

PSALM 119:125

2 TIMOTHY 2:7

WE HAVE CONFIDENCE IN THE HOLY SPIRIT WHO EMPOWERS US TO IMITATE JESUS CHRIST

STRUGGLES WITH SIN

We have all been marred by the curse of sinfulness. However, as believers, we have confidence in the Holy Spirit who empowers us to imitate Jesus Christ. We are admonished through Scripture to flee from our sinfulness and instead run to Jesus Christ. By confessing our sins, both to God and fellow believers, sin loses its grip over us.

When we willingly confess our sins and struggles, we can move forward, fleeing from sin and walking in obedience through the power of Jesus Christ.

STRUGGLES WITH SIN

I CORINTHIANS 6:19-20

I CORINTHIANS 10:13

EPHESIANS 4:22-24

GALATIANS 5:1

GALATIANS 5:16

I JOHN 1:8-10

JAMES 4:7

JOHN 15:5

PSALM 19:14

PSALM 40:11

PSALM 51:2

PSALM 51:10

ROMANS 6:13-14

2 TIMOTHY 2:22-23

HE PLUCKS US
FROM THE MIRE AND
GRANTS US HEALING
WHEN WE ASK

BITTERNESS

Bitterness easily takes deep roots in our souls. When we entertain bitterness, it can warp and distort our perspective, teaching us that Jesus cannot heal, reconcile, or enact justice. We lie to ourselves when we are bitter, not truly believing that Jesus Christ is sufficient for our happiness. We believe the lie that His sacrifice is not enough for us. But God doesn't leave us to wallow in bitterness. Instead, He plucks us from the mire and grants us healing when we ask for it. We don't have to cling to bitterness, hurt, or frustration. We can give these things to God, asking Him to bring beauty from the ugliness of bitterness. We can ask for His strength to extend the grace we have received.

There is freedom from bitterness, and it is found in an intimate understanding of the grace of God.

COLOSSIANS 3:12-14

EPHESIANS 4:31-32

HEBREWS 12:14-15

ISAIAH 5:20

I JOHN 2:9-11

I JOHN 4:8

LEVITICUS 19:18

LUKE 17:3-4

MARK 12:31

PROVERBS 10:12

PROVERBS 14:10

PROVERBS 20:22

ROMANS 3:23

ROMANS 12:17-21

IN HIM WE
FIND PEACE FOR
OUR UNREST

PEACE

We are creatures that crave the consolation of peace. Because of sin in the world, we often feel the effects of uncertainty, turbulence, and unrest. But we have given our lives over to the Prince of Peace, the author of goodness, and the giver of rest. In Him, we find peace for our unrest. Often our unrest comes from unpredictable circumstances. Thankfully, we serve an immutable God, unchanging in all of His ways. God is completely dependable and wholly trustworthy.

The peace that He gives us is lasting and reviving.
It will not wilt or fade away.

PEACE

2 CORINTHIANS 13:11

COLOSSIANS 3:15

ISAIAH 9:6

ISAIAH 26:3

ISAIAH 26:12

ISAIAH 55:12

1 PETER 3:11

1 PETER 5:7

PHILIPPIANS 4:7

PHILIPPIANS 4:9

PSALM 4:8

PSALM 29:11

PSALM 119:165

2 THESSALONIANS 3:16

WE ARE SONS
AND DAUGHTERS OF
THE MOST HIGH

INSECURITY & IDENTITY

When we accept Jesus Christ as our Savior and are sealed with the Holy Spirit inside of us, we no longer need to seek out our identity in the things of this world. In Christ, we no longer need job titles to fulfill us. We no longer need to be known by our quirks or by our appearance. When we are in Christ, we only ever need to be known as His. Our identity is not our own anymore, and insecurities no longer have a hold on our life. We are sons and daughters of the Most High, imitators of His divine Incarnation, and coheirs alongside Christ Himself. In Him, our identity is secure.

In Him, we are seen, we are loved, we are cherished, and we need no approval from the world.

EPHESIANS 1:5

EPHESIANS 2:10

GALATIANS 2:20

GENESIS 1:27

I JOHN 2:15

I JOHN 3:1-2

JEREMIAH 31:3

JOHN 1:12

JOHN 15:16

I PETER 2:9

PSALM 18:19

PSALM 139:14

ROMANS 8:37-39

ROMANS 12:2

I SAMUEL 16:7

WE KNOW
A GOD WHO
HEARS US

PRAYER

We know a God who hears us. Whether we come before Him to give thanks or to humbly request something, we can have confidence that He hears us. Even when we cannot express the words on our own, when we feel at a loss or can't communicate what's deeply held in our souls, we know that the Holy Spirit fills in our blanks. The Holy Spirit takes the words we cannot find and places them before God the Father on His throne. We are heard, whether we can muster the speech or not.

God always hears His children.

PRAYER

COLOSSIANS 4:2

HEBREWS 4:16

I JOHN 5:14-15

JAMES 5:13-14

JEREMIAH 29:12

JEREMIAH 33:3

JOHN 14:13

JUDE 20-21

LUKE 11:9

MARK 11:24

PSALM 34:17

PSALM 121

PSALM 141:2

PSALM 145:18-19

ROMANS 8:26-28

I THESSALONIANS 5:17

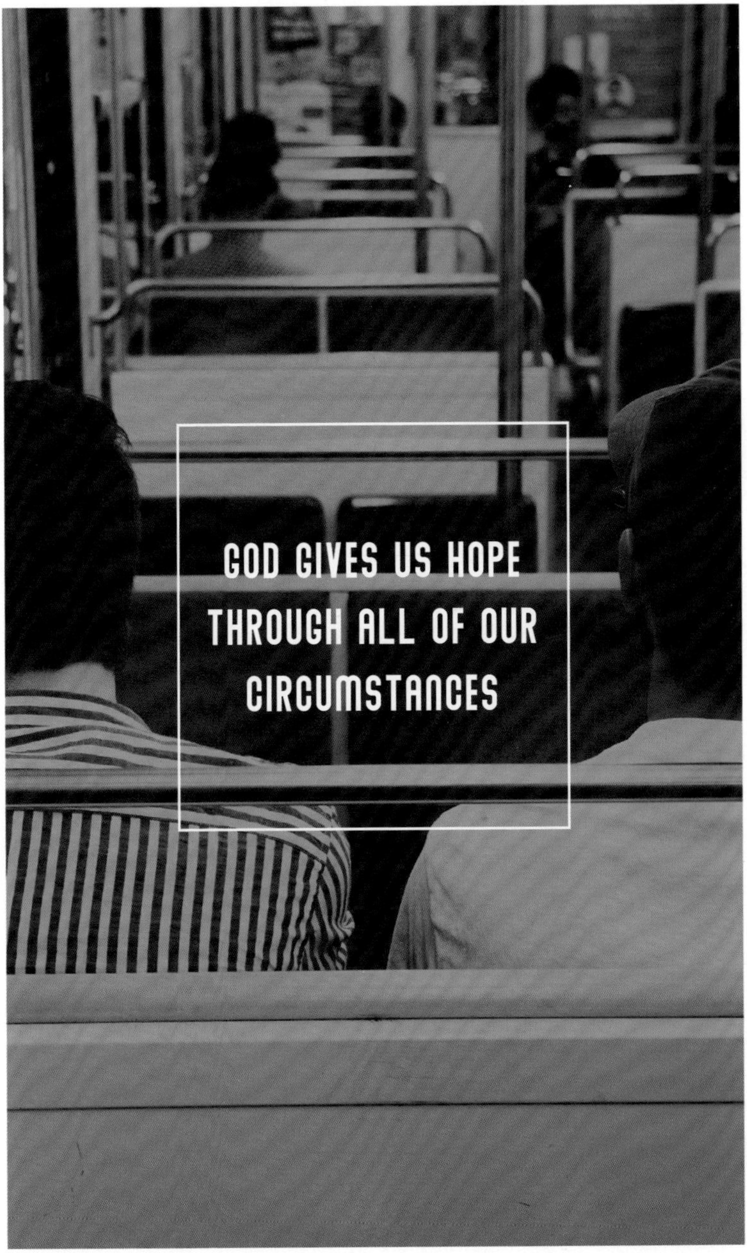

GOD GIVES US HOPE
THROUGH ALL OF OUR
CIRCUMSTANCES

HOPE

We have hope because we know that this world is not our permanent home. We have hope because we know that God is working out everything in our lives for our good and His glory. We have hope because God is good, and He is actively at work in this world to bring us closer to Him and to receive glory through it all. God gives us hope through all of our circumstances, no matter how dire they might be, because He is working to heal all things and make all things new.

Our hope is in the saving power of Jesus Christ's blood, knowing that God is at work to seek and save the lost so that we might all dwell in His presence in the new heaven and earth for all eternity.

I CORINTHIANS 13:13

2 CORINTHIANS 4:8-10

2 CORINTHIANS 4:17

HEBREWS 10:23

HEBREWS 11:1

PSALM 25:5

PSALM 31:24

PSALM 33:22

PSALM 42:11

PSALM 119:114

PSALM 130:5

ROMANS 5:2-4

WE MODEL OUR FORGIVENESS AFTER HIS ULTIMATE SACRIFICE ON OUR BEHALF

FORGIVENESS

Forgiveness always costs us something—it can cost us our pride, our selfishness, or our bitterness, but it cost Jesus Christ dying on the cross. We model our forgiveness after His ultimate sacrifice on our behalf. We experience the most scandalous forgiveness from Christ—He died so that we might live. His forgiveness is everlasting and permanent. We are called to forgive in the same radical way by forgiving those who grieve us, hurt us, and malign us.

God's profound forgiveness compels us to do the same for others, no matter what the offense is.

FORGIVENESS

COLOSSIANS 3:13

EPHESIANS 1:7

EPHESIANS 4:32

1 JOHN 1:9-10

JAMES 5:16

JOEL 2:13

MARK 11:25

MATTHEW 18:21-22

MATTHEW 6:14

MICAH 7:18

PSALM 86:5

PSALM 103:10-14

ROMANS 12:20

OUR GOD OFFERS FORTITUDE AND SAFETY

HELPLESSNESS

We are powerless and helpless on our own, but we serve a God who is all-powerful. The same God who breathed life into the cosmos has the power to uphold us and strengthen us in our seasons of helplessness. Our God offers fortitude and safety to us at all times. When we cannot seem to muster the strength to stand, when we cannot hold our head high and look to Heaven, when we are desperate and hurting, God is there to bear the load and uphold us for our good and for the sake of the task He has given us.

God is near and He is strong in all of our circumstances.

2 CORINTHIANS 12:9-10

EPHESIANS 3:16

EPHESIANS 6:10

HABAKKUK 3:19

ISAIAH 12:12

ISAIAH 40:29-31

MATTHEW 11:24

NEHEMIAH 8:10

PHILIPPIANS 4:13

PSALM 22:19

PSALM 28:7-8

PSALM 46:1

PSALM 118:14

ROMANS 5:6

IN HIM WE
ARE HOME

WEARINESS

The only place that we are truly able to find rest is in God. In Him, we find all that we need. In Him, we are home. He is the author and giver of all rest. His Word gives us refuge. Prayer brings us into a conversation with God Himself, uplifting our weary souls and refreshing our spirit. God alone can grant us the rest that we need and desire. The world cannot provide for us the true, pure rest that we crave. No matter how hard we search, whether in food, relationships, entertainment, or hobbies, nothing can give us rest like the Lord.

He energizes us, grants us strength, and uplifts our weary bones.

WEARINESS

EXODUS 33:14

GALATIANS 6:9

HEBREWS 12:3

ISAIAH 40:28-30

JEREMIAH 31:25

1 KINGS 8:56

MATTHEW 11:28-30

PSALM 26:3

PSALM 46:10

PSALM 62:1

PSALM 62:5

PSALM 73:26

PSALM 103

PSALM 119:28

HAVE FAITH IN
HIS GOODNESS

WAITING

Waiting on the Lord requires us to trust Him unceasingly. Waiting for Him to enact His plans requires us to be still and know that He is active and at work. It requires us to have faith in His goodness and to dwell on the riches of His grace. Waiting on the Lord teaches us to utilize our knowledge of His character, causing us to think about who He is and understand that He is dependable, trustworthy, true, perfect, loving, powerful, and wise. It causes us to look at who He is through new, vulnerable eyes.

In these seasons of waiting, God calls us to Himself to see and know and love Him in new and expanding ways.

I CORINTHIANS 15:58

COLOSSIANS 1:11

HOSEA 12:6

ISAIAH 30:18

ISAIAH 64:4

JAMES 1:12

LAMENTATIONS 3:25

MICAH 7:7

PSALM 5:3

PSALM 25:4-5

PSALM 27:13-14

PSALM 33:20

PSALM 130:5

ROMANS 12:12

HIS PLANS
WILL
NEVER FAIL

COURAGE

We are able to have courage, not because of our own actions or abilities, but because of our great God. He has proven Himself to us over and over again. He is a God who keeps His covenants with His people and who always enacts His plans perfectly. We have courage when we walk in obedience to His plan because His plans will never fail. When we experience fear, we can have the confidence to hand it over to God, knowing that He will always come through.

He will always provide, and He will always prevail.

COURAGE

I CORINTHIANS 15:58

I CORINTHIANS 16:13

DEUTERONOMY 31:6

EPHESIANS 6:13

ISAIAH 12:2

ISAIAH 41:10-13

ISAIAH 54:4

JOSHUA 1:9

PHILIPPIANS 4:13

PSALM 27:1

PSALM 31:24

PSALM 46:1

PSALM 56:3-4

PSALM 112:7

2 TIMOTHY 1:7

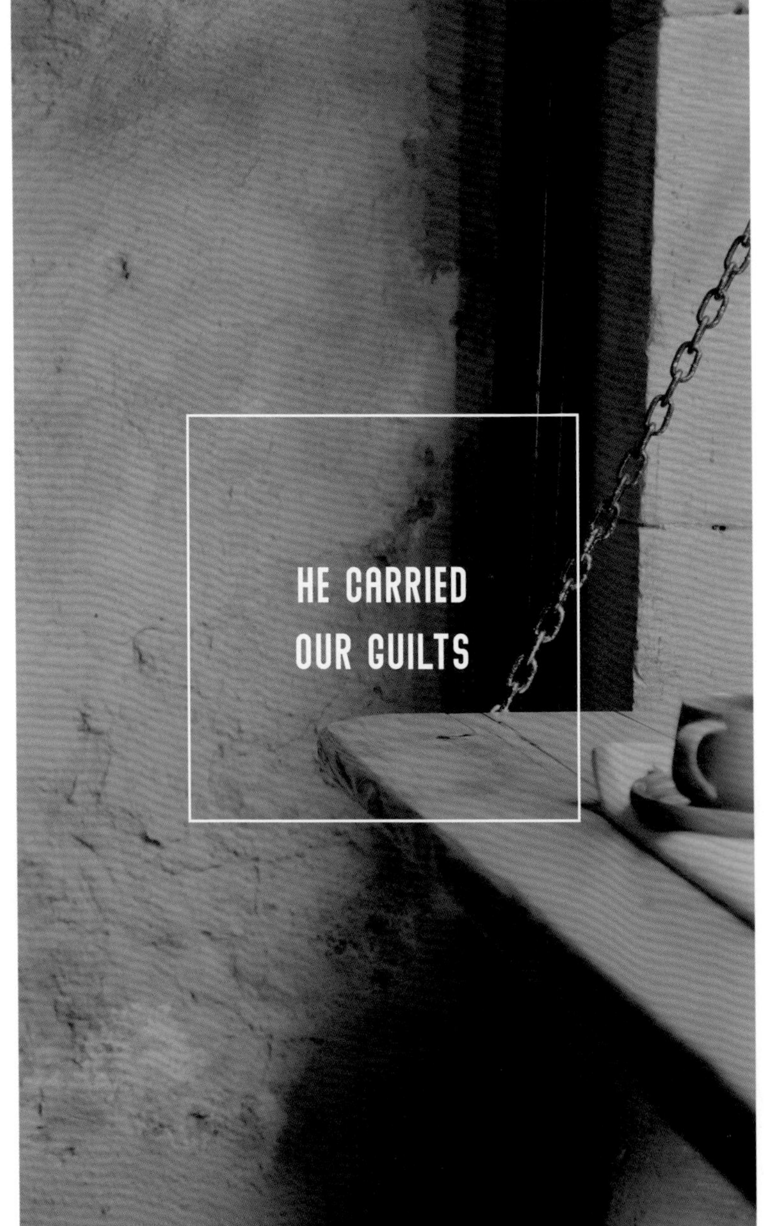
HE CARRIED
OUR GUILTS

GUILT

Jesus Christ came to the earth as a holy, perfect, sinless man, and He died on the cross and was raised from the dead for our sake. He died the death that we, as sinners, deserve. He bore the wrath of God on His shoulders and felt the weight of every sin that He paid for. Jesus Christ took on our guilt and shame, and He defeated it when He rose from the grave victoriously. He carried our guilt and gave us freedom. When we accept Christ as our Savior and pursue a relationship with Him, we are justified by His blood and made righteous by His sacrifice. Guilt no longer has power over us.

The blood of Jesus has covered it all.

2 CORINTHIANS 3:17

2 CORINTHIANS 5:17

2 CORINTHIANS 5:21

HEBREWS 8:12

ISAIAH 1:18

ISAIAH 43:25

JEREMIAH 33:8

JONAH 2:2

LUKE 15:7

PROVERBS 28:13

PSALM 103:11-12

PSALM 139:23-24

ROMANS 5:1

ROMANS 5:20-21

HE GRACIOUSLY
HOLDS US
TOGETHER

TRUST

People are not always trustworthy. We often may feel burned by our loved ones, but we can always trust the Lord. In every circumstance, with every difficult decision, with every ounce of suffering, God can be trusted. He graciously holds us together, bringing about His plans for our good and His glory. We can rest when we trust in Him. We can worship Him when we trust in Him. We can know and love Him better when we trust in Him.

Trusting the Lord is foundational to our faith—if we trust Him with our eternal security, can't we trust Him with the temporary things of this life?

TRUST

HEBREWS 11:6

ISAIAH 26:3-4

JOSHUA 23:14

PROVERBS 3:5-6

PSALM 13:5

PSALM 20:7

PSALM 37:3

PSALM 37:5-6

PSALM 40:4

PSALM 56:3

PSALM 84:12

PSALM 91

PSALM 118:8

ROMANS 15:13

THE LORD
ALONE IS RULER
OF ALL

PRIDE

The Bible speaks of pride often. Pride bubbles up when we begin to think of ourselves as our own god rather than keeping God in His proper place in our lives. Pride also surfaces when we think of ourselves as more important than others, when Scripture calls us to count others more significant than ourselves. Pride causes us to stumble in our walks with the Lord. It rots our faith and breaks relationships. The Word of God shows us a lot about how to avoid pride and the importance of doing so. When we flee from pride, we remind ourselves that the Lord alone is the Ruler of all.

When we flee from pride, we run toward God.

GALATIANS 6:1-3

JAMES 4:6

JAMES 4:10

MATTHEW 5:3

PHILIPPIANS 2:3

PROVERBS 11:2

PROVERBS 16:5

PROVERBS 26:12

PSALM 10:4

ROMANS 12:3

ROMANS 12:16

HE IS
GRACIOUSLY
PATIENT
WITH US

PATIENCE

God is all-knowing, and He is everywhere at once. He does not experience time in the same ways that we do. He is long-suffering, meaning He is graciously patient with us. This quality teaches us about patience and teaches us to trust in His divine timing. The Lord does not tarry. He is always on time, and all of His plans and works are perfectly timed.

Though we might grow restless in waiting for Him to work in our lives or answer our prayers, we can rest knowing that He is sovereign, He is in charge, and His timing is perfect.

PATIENCE

COLOSSIANS 3:12-13

ISAIAH 30:18

JAMES 5:7-8

LAMENTATIONS 3:26

2 PETER 3:8-9

PSALM 25:5

PSALM 27:14

PSALM 130:5

ROMANS 5:4

ROMANS 8:25

ROMANS 12:12

2 TIMOTHY 2:24

HE DOESN'T LEAVE
US TO SUFFER IN
OUR GRIEF ALONE

GRIEF

Grief can be a frightening and lonely experience. Praise God that He doesn't leave us to suffer in our grief alone. Instead, He provides us with hope. He gives us healing. He promises us the restoration of all things. There may not be a shortcut to experiencing freedom from grief, but we do know who holds the prescription: Jesus Christ. God grants us healing and peace. God gives us hope.

When grief seems like far too much to bear, and when the weight of it all lies heavily on our weary shoulders, we can preach to ourselves the truth that, in Jesus Christ, the broken are healed, and the grief-stricken are restored to a glorious hope.

2 CORINTHIANS 1:3-4

ISAIAH 41:10

ISAIAH 43:2

JOHN 14:1-4

LAMENTATIONS 3:31-33

MATTHEW 5:4

PSALM 34:18

PSALM 119:50

REVELATION 21:4

ROMANS 8:18

ROMANS 8:28

1 THESSALONIANS 4:13

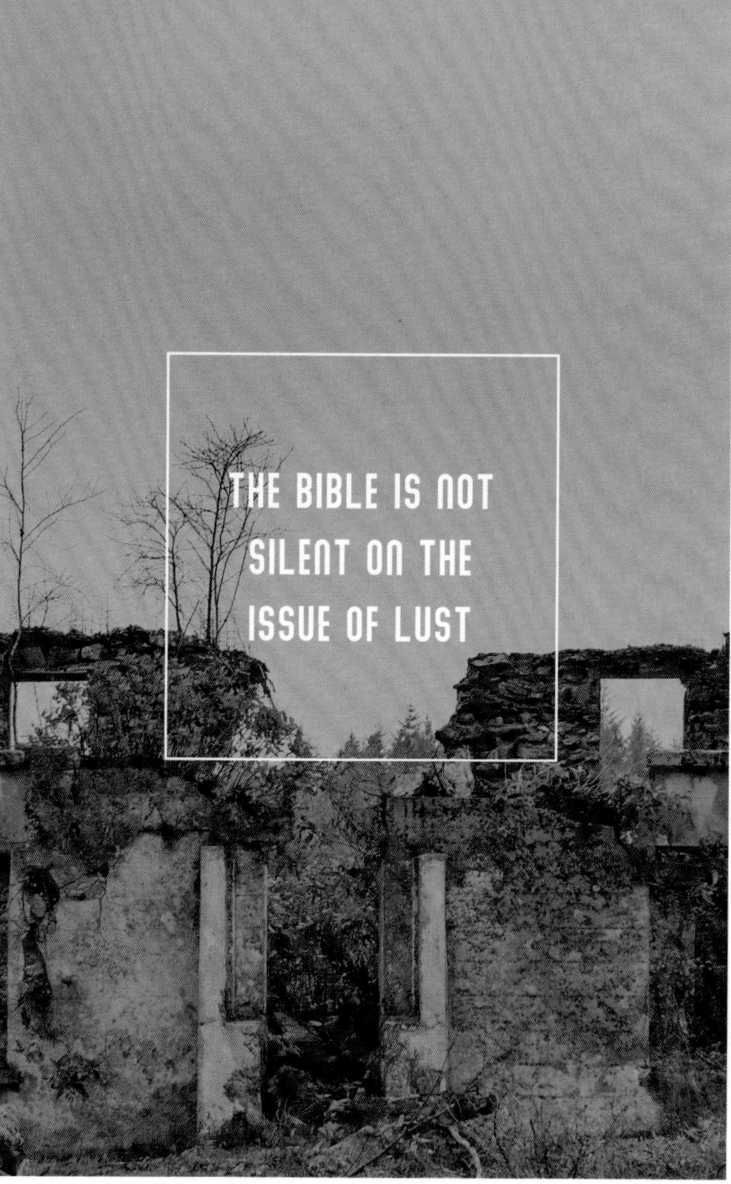
THE BIBLE IS NOT
SILENT ON THE
ISSUE OF LUST

LUST

We exist in a culture that celebrates lust. Advertisements, movies, and music are all filled with the objectification of fellow image-bearers. Indirectly through these means we're told that our bodies aren't worth much, and that other people are for our consumption. Thankfully, the Bible is not silent on the issue of lust. Scripture tells us over and over how we ought to value other humans, and more specifically, how we honor them by fleeing from lust. Lusting after others is a choice and is certainly something we have the propensity from which to abstain.

In wielding the sword of Scripture with the help of the Holy Spirit, we have hope to flee from lustful passions and cling to the Lord instead.

LUST

PSALM 119:9-11

MATTHEW 5:28

ROMANS 12:2

1 CORINTHIANS 10:13

GALATIANS 5:16

COLOSSIANS 3:5

1 THESSALONIANS 4:4-5

2 TIMOTHY 2:22

JAMES 1:14-15

1 PETER 2:11

1 JOHN 2:16

Thank you for studying God's Word with us

CONNECT WITH US

@thedailygraceco
@dailygracepodcast

CONTACT US

info@thedailygraceco.com

SHARE

#thedailygraceco

VISIT US ONLINE

www.thedailygraceco.com

MORE DAILY GRACE

The Daily Grace App
Daily Grace Podcast